# They Retired with Who?

## Revisiting players who ended their careers with unexpected teams

### By Jeff Wagner

**Also available:**

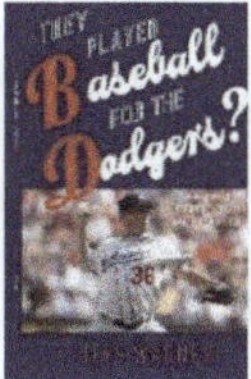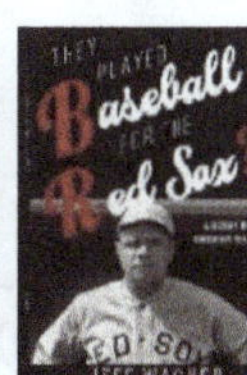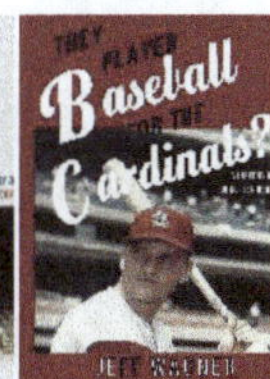

# Dedication

This book is dedicated to the memory of my father, Jim Wagner, who took me to my first professional basketball game in 1966, my first professional hockey game in 1969, my first professional baseball game in 1971, and my first professional football game in 1975. He not only introduced me to the world of sports, but instilled the importance of good sportsmanship and team work whenever playing one.

Also, to the memory of my sister Julie Martinez, who was probably a bigger local sports fan than I was!

And last but not least, I would also like to thank my loving wife Amy for her support, even though she has little to no interest in baseball. Thanks for the encouragement!

# Table of Contents


Introduction    1

Abbreviations Legend    2

**Major League Baseball**    3
  Babe Ruth – Boston Braves    3
  Billy Williams – Oakland A's    4
  Graig Nettles – Montreal Expos    5
  Duke Snider – San Francisco Giants    6
  Fernando Valenzuela – St. Louis Cardinals    7
  Frank Robinson – Cleveland Indians    8
  Gaylord Perry – Kansas City Royals    9
  Greg Maddux – Los Angeles Dodgers    10
  Hank Aaron – Milwaukee Brewers    11
  Harmon Killebrew – Kansas City Royals    12
  Juan Marichal – Los Angeles Dodgers    13
  Mike Piazza – Oakland A's    14
  Randy Johnson – San Francisco Giants    15
  Rickey Henderson – Los Angeles Dodgers    16
  Roger Maris – St. Louis Cardinals    17
  Ron Cey – Oakland A's    18
  Steve Carlton – Minnesota Twins    19
  Tom Seaver – Boston Red Sox    20
  Ty Cobb – Philadelphia A's    21
  Warren Spahn – San Francisco Giants    22
  Willie Mays – New York Mets    23
  Yogi Berra – New York Mets    24

**National Football League**    25
  Alan Page – Chicago Bears    25
  Carl Eller – Seattle Seahawks    26
  Deacon Jones – Washington Redskins    27
  Don Maynard – Los Angeles Rams    28
  Earl Campbell – New Orleans Saints    29
  Emmitt Smith – Arizona Cardinals    30
  Franco Harris – Seattle Seahawks    31
  Jerry Rice – Denver Broncos    32
  Joe Montana – Kansas City Chiefs    33
  Joe Namath – Los Angeles Rams    34
  Johnny Unitas – San Diego Chargers    35

Ken Stabler – New Orleans Saints 36
Lance Alworth – Dallas Cowboys 37
Randy Moss – San Francisco 49ers 38
Reggie White – Carolina Panthers 39
Ronnie Lott – Kansas City Chiefs 40
Tim Brown – Tampa Bay Buccaneers 41
Tony Dorsett – Denver Broncos 42

**National Basketball Association** **43**
Bob Cousy – Cincinnati Royals 43
Dominique Wilkins – Orlando Magic 44
George Gervin – Chicago Bulls 45
Hakeem Olajuwon – Toronto Raptors 46
Karl Malone – Los Angeles Lakers 47
Michael Jordan – Washington Wizards 48
Nate Thurmond – Cleveland Cavaliers 49
Patrick Ewing – Orlando Magic 50
Rick Barry – Houston Rockets 51
Shaquille O'Neal – Boston Celtics 52
Walt Frazier – Cleveland Cavaliers 53
Wilt Chamberlain – San Diego Conquistadors 54

**National Hockey League** **55**
Bobby Hull – Hartford Whalers 55
Bobby Orr – Chicago Blackhawks 56
Chris Chelios – Atlanta Thrashers 57
Eric Lindros – Dallas Stars 58
Gordie Howe – Hartford Whalers 59
Guy Lafleur – Quebec Nordiques 60
Jaromír Jágr – Calgary Flames 61
Larry Robinson – Los Angeles Kings 63
Paul Coffey – Boston Bruins 64
Ray Bourque – Colorado Avalanche 65
Wayne Gretzky – New York Rangers 66

**Primary Book Sources** **68**

**Author's Bio** **69**

**More Books from the Author** **70**

## Introduction

Many players throughout sports history are identified with one team. Babe Ruth and the Yankees, Willie Mays and the Giants, Jerry Rice and the 49ers, Johnny Unitas and the Colts, Michael Jordan and the Bulls, and Bobby Orr and the Bruins. But, amazing as it may seem, none of these players ended their careers with those teams.

And they aren't the only ones, as you'll see when we examine 60 players from Major League Baseball (MLB), the National Basketball Association (NBA), the National Football League (NFL) and the National Hockey League (NHL) who ended their careers with teams that you may not have expected.

And we're talking big names: Ruth, Snider, Spahn, Cobb, Seaver, Killebrew, Namath, Montana, Chamberlain, Ewing, Malone, Hull, Howe, Gretzky, and many others.

So enjoy as we look back at some of the greats in professional sports history!

## Abbreviations Legend

The following abbreviations are used throughout this book:

- MLB:     Major League Baseball
- NL:      National League
- AL:      American League
- NFL:     National Football League
- AFL:     American Football League
- NFC:     National Football Conference
- AFC:     American Football Conference
- NBA:     National Basketball Association
- ABA:     American Basketball Association
- NCAA:    National Collegiate Athletic Association
- NHL:     National Hockey League
- WHL:     World Hockey League
- MVP:     Most Valuable Player
- RBI:     Runs Batted In
- ERA:     Earned Run Average

# Major League Baseball

## Babe Ruth – Boston Braves

CAREER HIGHLIGHTS

- Hall of Fame
- 1x MVP
- 12x Home Run leader
- 5x RBI leaders
- 1x Batting title
- 1x ERA title
- 2x 20 game winner

George Herman Ruth played his first professional game on March 7, 1914 with the minor league Baltimore Orioles of the International League. By June 1914, Orioles owner Jack Dunn was forced to sell his players because of financial hardship, and sold Ruth's contract to the Boston Red Sox on July 4, 1914.

In 1919, with his salary demands being deemed excessive, Red Sox owner Harry Frazee decided to sell Ruth to the New York Yankees for a then whopping $125,000. In the 12 seasons between 1920 and 1931 with the Yankees, Ruth led the American League in slugging 11 times, home runs 10 times, walks nine times, on-base percentage eight times, and runs scored seven times. His batting average topped .350 eight times.

### BECOMING A BRAVE

In 1935, Yankees owner Jacob Ruppert had no interest in the 40-year-old Ruth returning to the team, and worked out a deal with Boston Braves owner Emil Fuchs. Fuchs would offer Ruth a contract that included the titles of "assistant manager" and "vice president". Ruth ended up playing in 28 games for the Braves in 1935, batting .181. His last hurrah would be on May 25 in Pittsburgh, when he belted the final three home runs of his career while driving in six runs. After trips to Cincinnati and Philadelphia, Ruth would retire on June 2.

## Billy Williams – Oakland A's

Career Highlights

- Hall of Fame
- Rookie of the Year
- 6x All-Star
- 1x Batting Title
- 1x Hits Leader
- 1x Runs Scored Leader

Billy Leo Williams played 14 of his 16 years with the Chicago Cubs, winning National League rookie-of-the-year in 1961. A six-time All-Star, Williams was the second most durable player in National League history, playing 1,117 consecutive games at one point, and was elected to the National Baseball Hall of Fame in 1987.

### Becoming an Athletic

In 1974, the Cubs finished in last place with their worst record since 1966. After two years of declining production, the 37 year-old Williams was traded after the 1974 season to the Oakland Athletics for Manny Trillo, Darold Knowles, and Bob Locker.

Rebounding as a designated hitter, Williams hit 23 homers with 81 RBI in 1975 for the A's, and on June 12 became the 16th player to hit 400 career home runs when he homered in a 9-7 loss at Milwaukee against the Brewers. In the postseason that year, Williams went hitless in seven at bats. After hitting .211 in 120 games for the A's in 1976, Williams retired following his last major league game on October 2, picking up a single in his final plate appearance in a 14-inning, 9-8 win over the California Angels.

Sadly, Williams never had a chance to play in a World Series in his career, just missing out with the A's, who had won the three previous World Series prior to his joining them in 1975.

## Graig Nettles – Montreal Expos

CAREER HIGHLIGHTS

- 6x All-Star
- 2x Golden Glove
- 2x World Series
- 1x AL Home Run leader
- ALCS MVP

Graig "Puff" Nettles played for the Minnesota Twins, Cleveland Indians, New York Yankees, San Diego Padres, Atlanta Braves, and Montreal Expos during his 22-year baseball career. Regarded as one of the best defensive third basemen of all time, Nettles won two Gold Glove Awards in 1977 and 1978. His career statistics include 2,225 hits, 390 home runs, and 1,314 RBIs. With the Yankees, Nettles was a six-time All-Star and won two World Series championships in 1977 and 1978.

After 11 seasons with the Yankees, the 38 year-old Nettles informed the team that he wished to play closer to home in San Diego. So on March 30, 1984, the Yankees traded Nettles to the Padres for pitcher Dennis Rasmussen. San Diego would go to the World Series that year, only to lose to the Detroit Tigers in five games. After the 1986 season, the Padres declined to offer Nettles a contract, making him a free agent. Nettles signed with the Atlanta Braves for the 1987 season and re-signed with them for 1988.

### BECOMING AN EXPO

On March 24, 1988, the Braves sold Nettles to the Montreal Expos. In Montreal, Nettles had 93 at-bats in 80 games, batting .172 while hitting one home run and driving in 14 runs. He retired after the season at the age of 43.

## Duke Snider – San Francisco Giants

CAREER HIGHLIGHTS

- Hall of Fame
- 8x All-Star
- 1x Home Run leader
- 1x RBI leader
- 1x Hits leader
- 3x Runs Scored leader

Debuting in 1947 with the Brooklyn Dodgers, Edwin Donald "Duke" Snider quickly established himself as one of the league's best outfielders, becoming a key player in the team's success during the 1950s, forming part of the iconic trio alongside Jackie Robinson and Roy Campanella. This period marked the golden age of the Dodgers, as they won several National League pennants and the 1955 World Series.

Snider would hit .295, belt 407 home runs and drive in 1,333 runs during an 18 career. He also collected 2,116 hits to become the seventh player in history to have 400 home runs and 2,000 hits. He was an eight-time All-Star and led the league in home runs (1956) and RBIs (1955), hits (1950), and runs scored (1953-55) during his career.

BECOMING A GIANT

After hitting .278 with five home runs and 30 RBIs in 80 games for the Dodgers in 1962, the 35-year old returned to New York the following year when he was sold to the expansion Mets. After one year in New York in which the Mets would lose 111 games, Snider asked to be traded to a contender. So on April 14, 1964, he was sold to his former arch-rival San Francisco Giants who were battling for the National League pennant. Snider would play in 91 games and hit .210 with four home runs and 17 RBIs before retiring as a Giant at season's end.

## Fernando Valenzuela – St. Louis Cardinals

CAREER HIGHLIGHTS

- 1x Cy Young
- Rookie of the Year
- 6x All Star
- 1x Wins leader
- 1x Strike Out leader

Fernando Valenzuela debuted with the Los Angeles Dodgers in 1980, earning both the NL Rookie of the Year and Cy Young Awards that year. He would be a key player for the Dodgers for the next 10 seasons.

In the spring of 1991, after four seasons with a record of .500 or below, Valenzuela was released by the Dodgers and picked up by the California Angels. Just over a month later, after two starts and an ERA over 12.00, he was released again. In 1992 he was signed by the Detroit Tigers, but his contract was sold to the Jalisco Charros in Mexico before he even appeared in a game for the Tigers. He would go 10-9 for Jalisco with a 3.86 ERA.

Valenzuela would return to the Major Leagues in 1993 with the Baltimore Orioles, going 8-10 with a 4.94 ERA. He would sign with the Philadelphia Phillies in 1994 and pitch eight games before signing with the San Diego Padres in the spring of 1995. He pitched for the Padres for 2 1/2 seasons, making an impressive comeback in 1996 with a 13-8 record and a 3.62 ERA.

BECOMING A CARDINAL

After a 2-8 start with the Padres in 1997, Valenzuela was traded mid-season with two players to the St. Louis Cardinals for Rich Batchelor, Danny Jackson and Mark Sweeney. He went 0-4 in five starts for the Cards and was released after a month with the club, ending his major league career on June 13, 1997 at the age of 36 with 172 wins, a 3.54 ERA, and 2,074 strikeouts.

## Frank Robinson – Cleveland Indians

CAREER HIGHLIGHTS

- Hall of Fame
- Rookie of the Year
- 2x MVP
- 14x All Ster
- 1x Batting Title
- 1x Triple Crown

Frank Robinson began his MLB career with the Cincinnati Reds in 1956 winning the Rookie of the Year award that year, and five years later capturing the NL MVP award when he hit .323 with 37 home runs and 124 RBIs.

In 1966, Robinson was traded to the Baltimore Orioles in what is regarded as one of MLB's worst trades ever, as the Reds received little known pitchers Jack Baldschun, Milt Pappas and Dick Simpson in return. In his first season with the Orioles, Robinson hit for the triple crown while winning his second MVP to accomplish the rare feat of winning the MVP award in both leagues. Robinson played an important role in leading the Orioles to their first World Series championship that same year and again in 1970.

BECOMING AN INDIAN

On September 12, 1974, after two productive seasons with the California Angels, the halos traded Robinson to the Cleveland Indians, who three weeks later would name him their manager while persuading him to continue playing. In his first at bat as a player/manager for Cleveland in 1975, Robinson hit a home run off of Doc Medich of the New York Yankees. In just over two years, Robinson played in 100 games hitting .226 with 14 home runs and 39 RBIs, mostly as a designated hitter, while leading the team to two fourth place finishes as their manager. Robinson retired as a player with Cleveland following the 1976 season at the age of 40, finishing with 586 home runs.

## Gaylord Perry – Kansas City Royals

**CAREER HIGHLIGHTS**

- Hall of Fame
- 2x Cy Young
- 5x All-Star
- 3x Wins leader

Gaylord Jackson Perry's MLB career began with the San Francisco Giants in 1962 and he quickly gained a reputation as a reliable and crafty pitcher. Particularly known for his diverse repertoire of pitches, including an alleged spitball, Perry's career spanned 22 seasons during which he played for eight different teams.

On May 6, 1982 with the Seattle Mariners, Perry hurled a complete game 7-3 victory over the Yankees for his 300th win, becoming the first 300-game-winner since Early Wynn in 1963. Perry finished the season 10-12 with a 4.40 ERA over 32 starts and 216⅔ innings.

On August 23 that season, Perry was first warned, then ejected, by plate umpire Dave Phillips for throwing two allegedly "illegal" pitches. It was the first and only time Perry had been kicked out of a ballgame for his "famous" pitch.

### BECOMING A ROYAL

Perry finally wound down in 1983, going 3-10 with the Mariners before drawing his release on June 27, and then finishing 4-4 with the Kansas City Royals who signed him a week later. At the end of the 1983 season, Perry retired from baseball at the age of 44. His 314 wins were good for 11th on the all-time list at the time, and his 3,534 strikeouts placed him third.

## Greg Maddux – Los Angeles Dodgers

**CAREER HIGHLIGHTS**

- Hall of Fame
- 4x Cy Young
- 8x All-Star
- 18x Gold Gloves
- 4x ERA title
- 3x Wins leader

During his time with the Chicago Cubs and Atlanta Braves, Gregory Alan Maddux played in eight All-Star games, while winning four consecutive Cy Young awards. He also led the league in wins three times, ERA four times, games started eight times, innings pitched five times, and won 18 Gold Glove awards for his fielding.

**BECOMING AN DODGER**

On July 31, 2006, the 40 year-old Maddux was traded for the first time in his career, when the Chicago Cubs sent him to the Los Angeles Dodgers for Cesar Izturis. In his first Dodger start, Maddux threw six no-hit innings before being interrupted by a rain delay. With 15 wins in 2006 (6-3 with the Dodgers), Maddux finished in the league's Top 10 in wins for the 18th time, breaking the record of 17 he had shared with Cy Young and Warren Spahn.

After signing a free-agent contract with the San Diego Padres for 2007, Maddux was traded back to the Dodgers on August 19, 2008 after going 6-9 in 26 starts with San Diego. After pitching four innings of relief in the 2008 post season for Los Angeles, Maddux would announce his retirement, finishing his career with 355 wins, eighth best all-time.

## Hank Aaron – Milwaukee Brewers

**CAREER HIGHLIGHTS**

- Hall of Fame
- 1x MVP
- 25x All-Star
- 4x Home Run leader
- 4x RBI leaders
- 2x Batting Title

In 1957, Henry Louis Aaron played a pivotal role in leading the Milwaukee Braves to their first and only World Series title, earning him widespread recognition. On May 17, 1970, Aaron recorded his 3,000th career hit off Reds pitcher Wayne Simpson with a single in the second game of a doubleheader in Cincinnati, becoming the first player to reach that milestone while hitting 500 career home runs. Aaron's most iconic moment came on April 8, 1974, when he surpassed Babe Ruth's long-standing home run record by hitting his 715th career home run. On October 2nd, Aaron hit his 733rd and final home run as a Brave in his last at-bat with the team.

### BECOMING A BREWER

At the end of the 1974 season, with his contract with the Braves at an end, Aaron requested a trade to the Milwaukee Brewers, due to a prior relationship with Brewer owner, Bud Selig. On November 2nd, the Braves traded the 41-year old to the Brewers for Roger Alexander and Dave May, after which he would sign a two-year contract. Because the Brewers were an American League team, Aaron could extend his career by becoming a designated hitter. Plus it gave him the opportunity to end his career in the city where it began some 20 years earlier.

Aaron broke baseball's all-time RBI record on May 1, 1975 and, on July 20, 1976, hit his 755th and final home run off the California Angels' Dick Drago in Milwaukee. Aaron played in 222 games for the Brewers hitting .232 with 22 home runs and 95 RBIs.

## Harmon Killebrew – Kansas City Royals

**CAREER HIGHLIGHTS**

- Hall of Fame
- 1x MVP
- 13x All-Star
- 6x Home Run leader
- 3x RBI leaders

One of the most prolific power hitters in MLB history, Killebrew hit 20 or more home runs in a season 13 times, 30 or more 10 times, and 40 or more eight times. Nine times he would drive in 100 or more runs in a season. He would collect 1,584 RBIs in 2,086 hits, or an impressive average of one RBI every 1.31 at-bats.

In December 1974, after 21 seasons with the franchise and at the end of his current contract, the 38-year old Killebrew was given the option of staying with the Twins as a coach and batting instructor, managing the AAA Tacoma Twins, or being released. He chose to be released.

**BECOMING A ROYAL**

On January 24, 1975, eight days after getting his release, Killebrew signed a one-year contract with the Kansas City Royals. During his return to Minnesota in early May, the Twins formally retired his No. 3 jersey. In that game, Killebrew hit a home run against his former teammates and received a standing ovation from the crowd. In 106 games with the Royals, he batted .199 with 14 home runs and 44 RBIs. At the end of the season, the Royals released Killebrew. In March 1976, he formally announced his retirement, finishing fifth on the all-time home run list with 573.

## Juan Marichal – Los Angeles Dodgers

CAREER HIGHLIGHTS

- Hall of Fame
- 2x Wins leader
- 10x All-Star
- 1x ERA title
- 1x NL Pitching title

During the 1960's, Juan Marichal's 191 wins was 27 more than second place Bob Gibson. His 2.57 ERA was bettered only by Sandy Koufax's 2.36. He was third in innings pitched and his 45 shutouts led the decade by four over Gibson. In addition, Marichal won 20 games in six seasons over an eight year period that decade, including four in a row.

After 14 years in San Francisco, the Giants sold the struggling 35 year-old's contract to the Boston Red Sox on December 8, 1973. Although going 5–1 in 11 starts for Boston, but with a lofty 4.87 ERA, Marichal was released after the season.

### BECOMING A DODGER

On March 15, 1975, Marichal signed with the once arch-rival Los Angeles Dodgers, to the displeasure of many Dodger fans who hadn't forgiven Marichal for the infamous "bat" incident with John Roseboro 10 years earlier. It took a personal appeal from Roseboro himself, who by that time was good friends with Marichal, to help calm things down. Marichal's 1975 was short-lived, however, as he gave up nine runs, 11 hits and posted a 13.50 ERA in only two starts before retiring following his last outing on April 16.

Marichal finished his career with 243 victories, 142 losses, 244 complete games, 2,303 strikeouts and a 2.89 ERA over 3,507 innings pitched.

## Mike Piazza – Oakland A's

Career Highlights

- Hall of Fame
- Rookie of the Year
- 12x All-Star

One of the best offensive catchers in baseball history, Michael Joseph Piazza hit over .300 ten times during his 16 year career, finishing with a .308 lifetime average. He also hit over 20 home runs in 12 of those years, and over 30 nine times. He was drafted in the 62nd round of baseball's 1988 Amateur Draft, as a favor to Piazza's father, who was a close friend of Los Angeles Dodgers manager Tommy Lasorda, both of whom were born in Norristown, Pennsylvania.

After batting .362 with 40 home runs in 1997, the Dodgers offered Piazza a six-year, $80 million contract, which he turned down in order to test the free agent market at the end of the season. Before that could happen, however, the Dodgers sent Piazza and Todd Zeile to the Florida Marlins for Gary Sheffield, Charles Johnson, Bobby Bonilla, Jim Eisenreich, and Manuel Barrios in May 15, 1998. A week later, Piazza was traded to the New York Mets for Preston Wilson, Ed Yarnall, and Geoff Goetz, shocking the media and fans.

Following his stints in Miami and New York, Piazza returned to the West Coast in 2006, signing a one-year, $1.25 million contract with the San Diego Padres.

Becoming an athletic

After batting .283 with 22 home runs and 68 RBIs with the Padres, Piazza signed a one-year, $8.5 million contract with the Oakland A's for 2007. A shoulder injury in early May that year led to an 11-week stay on the disabled list, after which Piazza finished the season with a .275 average, hitting eight home runs, and driving in 44 runs. He would retire after the season at the age of 38.

## Randy Johnson – San Francisco Giants

**CAREER HIGHLIGHTS**

- Hall of Fame
- 3x Cy Young
- 10x All-Star
- 9x Strikeout title
- 4x ERA title

Randall David Johnson's 303 career victories rank as the fifth-most by a left-hander in Major League Baseball history, while his 4,875 strikeouts place him first for lefties and second all-time behind Nolan Ryan. On May 18, 2004, the 40 year-old Johnson became the oldest pitcher in Major League Baseball history to throw a perfect game. He is also one of eighteen pitchers in history to record a win against all 30 franchises.

After logging an 11–10 record and 3.91 ERA during a 2008 season which saw Randy Johnson record his 100th career complete game, the Arizona Diamondbacks waived the 45-year old free agent on November 13, 2008, just five wins short of the magical 300 number.

### BECOMING A GIANT

On December 26, 2008, Johnson signed a one-year deal with the San Francisco Giants in his quest to become the twenty-fourth pitcher in MLB history to reach 300 wins. And on June 4, 2009, he did just that, beating the Washington Nationals 5-1 at Nationals Park.

Less than two months later, however, Johnson was placed on the 60-day disabled list with a torn rotator cuff in his throwing shoulder. On September 16, Johnson was activated and assigned to the Giants bullpen, and three days later made his first relief appearance in four years. Four months after the season ended, on January 5, 2010, Johnson announced his retirement from professional baseball. During his single season with the Giants, Johnson went 8-6 with a 4.88 ERA in 22 games, striking out 86 hitters in 96 innings.

## Rickey Henderson – Los Angeles Dodgers

**CAREER HIGHLIGHTS**

- Hall of Fame
- 1x AL MVP
- 12x Stolen base leader
- 10x All-Star
- 5x Runs Scored leader
- 1x Hits leader

Arguably the greatest lead-off hitter in MLB history, Rickey Nelson Henley Henderson would rank first all time in runs scored with 2,295, in stolen bases with 1,406 and leadoff home runs with 81 after playing his last Major League game in 2003. He also ranked second all-time in walks (2,190) and 26th in hits (3,055). For his career, he clouted 297 home runs, drove in 1,115 RBIs, and hit .279. Henderson stole a record 130 bases in 1982, and his 1,406 career total is 468 ahead of second place Lou Brock's 938.

### BECOMING A DODGER

As the 2003 season began, Henderson was without a team for the first time in his 24 year career. The year before, he had signed a minor league contract with the Boston Red Sox, but after 72 games, the Red Sox released him in mid-2002. Prior to the 2003 season, Henderson signed with the Newark Bears in the independent Atlantic League, hoping for a chance with another major league organization. The opportunity came on July 14, 2003 when Henderson signed on with the Los Angeles Dodgers.

In 30 games with the Dodgers, his ninth and final team, he collected 15 hits, three stolen bases and a .208 batting average. Henderson played his last major league game on September 19, 2003 and was hit by a pitch in his only plate appearance. He would go around to score his 2,295th run, tops in Major League Baseball history.

## Roger Maris – St. Louis Cardinals

CAREER HIGHLIGHTS

- 7x All-Star
- 2x MVP
- 1x Home Run leader
- 2x RBI leaders

Roger Eugene Maris began his career with the Cleveland Indians and Kansas City Athletics before being traded to the New York Yankees by the A's in a six player deal on December 11, 1959.

Maris was an immediate hit in New York, winning back-to-back AL MVP Awards in 1960 and 1961, leading the league in RBIs both seasons. In 1961, Maris made baseball history by clubbing 61 home runs to eclipse Babe Ruth's long standing record of 60.

### BECOMING A CARDINAL

A struggling Yankee team decided to cut salary after the 1966 season, and traded an equally struggling Maris to the St. Louis Cardinals for journeyman third baseman Charley Smith. Maris had hit .233 with 13 homers and 43 RBIs in 1966.

Though Maris played only two years in St. Louis, he helped the Cardinals to back-to-back World Series, the first an exciting seven-game 1967 win over the Boston Red Sox and the second the following year in an equally exciting seven game loss to the Detroit Tigers. Maris hit .385 with one home run and seven RBIs in the series against Boston.

Limited by injuries, Maris decided to retire after the 1968 season at the age of 33.

## Ron Cey – Oakland A's

Career Highlights

- Hall of Fame
- 1x MVP
- 12x Home Run leader
- 5x RBI leaders
- 1x Batting Title
- 1x ERA Title
- 2x 20 game winner

Ronald Charles "Penguin" Cey would spend his first 12 years in baseball as a Los Angeles Dodger, playing in four Word Series and six All-Star games before being traded to the Chicago Cubs after the 1982 season for Dan Cataline and Vance Lovelace, despite hitting 24 home runs and driving in 79.

In four seasons with the Cubs, Cey helped lead them to the National League East Division title in 1984, hitting 25 homers and driving in 97 runs, both team highs. In 1985, the 37-year-old's batting average dipped to .232, although he still hit 22 home runs with 63 RBIs in 145 games.

### Becoming an Athletic

After his playing time dropped to 97 games in 1986 with the Cubs, Cey was traded to the Oakland Athletics for utility infielder Luis Quinones in January 1987, and joined former nemesis Reggie Jackson for 45 games. On July 15, 1987, after hitting just .211 with four home runs and 11 RBIs, the A's would release Cey, who would retire soon after at the age of 39, ending 17 years of pro ball.

## Steve Carlton – Minnesota Twins

### Career Highlights

- Hall of Fame
- 4x Cy Young
- 10x All-Star
- 1x ERA Title
- 4x 20 game winner

Between 1971 and 1982, Steven Norman "Lefty" Carlton was a 20-game winner six times, a Cy Young winner four times, and an All-Star 10 times. In 1972, Carlton had one of the most amazing years in baseball history for a hurler when he pitched a whopping 346 innings, won 27 games, and posted a 1.97 ERA. And all for a Philadelphia Phillies team that only won 57 games all year.

Fast forward to 1986, where the lefty's ERA had steadily been climbing since 1982. On June 24, the Phillies released Carlton, who signed with the San Francisco Giants ten days later. After an unproductive month, Carlton was again released, but not before striking out his 4,000[th] batter to become the second pitcher to do so. Carlton would finish the season with the Chicago White Sox, before signing with the Cleveland Indians at the start of the 1987 season where he made history when he and Phil Niekro became the first teammates with 300 wins to appear in the same game..

### Becoming a Twin

On July 31, 1987, the Indians traded Carlton to the Minnesota Twins. Nine days later, he got his 329th and final victory as the Twins defeated the Oakland A's, 9-2. The Twins would win the World Series that year, giving Carlton his first ring since 1967 with the Cardinals.

Carlton was released by the Twins on April 28, 1988 after four games when he went 0-1 with a 16.76 ERA.

## Tom Seaver – Boston Red Sox

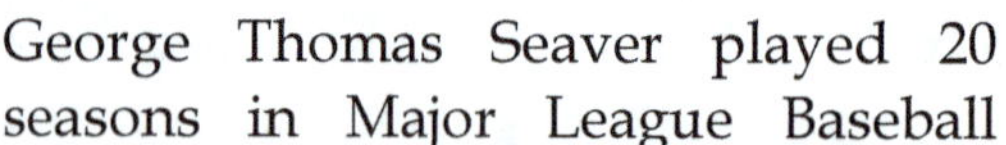

**C**AREER **H**IGHLIGHTS

- Hall of Fame
- Rookie of the Year
- 3x Cy Young
- 3x Wins leader
- 3x ERA title
- 12x All-Star

George Thomas Seaver played 20 seasons in Major League Baseball beginning in 1967, primarily for the New York Mets, leading them to their first World Series title in 1969. A 12-time All-Star, he won three Cy Young Awards and recorded 311 career victories.

In 1986 with the Chicago White Sox, Seaver started on Opening Day for the 16th and final time of his career.

### B**ECOMING A** R**ED** S**OCK**

In the middle of the 1986 season, the White Sox traded Seaver to the pennant-contending Boston Red Sox for Steve Lyons. Seaver would go 5–7 with a 3.80 earned run average in 16 starts in his only season with Boston, getting his 311th and final win on August 18, 1986 against the Minnesota Twins. A knee injury would prevent Seaver from facing his old team, the New York Mets, in the World Series that year. The Red Sox did not offer Seaver a contract to his liking for the 1987 season, declining the Red Sox offer of $500,000. With no new contract agreement reached, Seaver was granted free agency on November 12, 1986.

Seaver tried to put on uniform number 41 for the Mets one last time in 1987, but after joining the club on June 6 was hit hard in an exhibition game against the Triple-A Tidewater Tides five days later. After similarly poor outings on June 16 and 20, he announced his retirement at age 42.

## Ty Cobb – Philadelphia A's

**CAREER HIGHLIGHTS**

- Hall of Fame
- 1x MVP
- 12x Batting titles
- 1x Triple Crown
- 8x Hits leader
- 1x Home Run leader
- 4x RBI leader

Tyrus Raymond Cobb, nicknamed "the Georgia Peach", spent 22 seasons with the Detroit Tigers, the last six as the team's player-manager. In 1926, the Tigers fell to sixth place in the American League, but still had a respectable 79-75 record. Nevertheless, Cobb surprised the baseball world by announcing that he was stepping down as manager of the Tigers and retiring from baseball on November 3, 1926.

### BECOMING AN ATHLETIC

In February 1927, Cobb received a lucrative offer from Philadelphia owner and manager Connie Mack, one of the few men in baseball that Cobb truly admired and respected, Cobb agreed to join the Athletics, playing with the club for two seasons before announcing his final retirement.

In his two seasons with the A's, Cobb hit .343 in 228 games at 40 and 41 years of age, mostly at first base. Amazingly, his .343 average was 23 points below his career average of .366.

When he retired, Cobb was MLB's all-time leader in hits (4,189), runs scored (2,244), and stolen bases (897). He holds the major league record for most hits with one club, 3,900 as a member of the Detroit Tigers. Finishing with a .366 career batting average, Cobb hit over .300 in 23 consecutive seasons when he retired, with the only season he didn't being his rookie year. He hit over .400 twice in his career.

## Warren Spahn – San Francisco Giants

CAREER HIGHLIGHTS

- Hall of Fame
- 17x All-Star
- 8x Win titles
- 3x ERA titles
- 4x Strikeout leader
- 1x Cy Young

In 23 seasons, most with the Milwaukee Braves, Warren Edward Spahn won 363 games; winning 20 or more games 13 times; while hitting 35 career home runs.

From the age of 35 through 40, Spahn won 20 or more games each season. At the age of 42, he won 23 games and pitched a complete 15 inning, 201 pitch game that year in which he lost to the Giants and Juan Marichal, 1-0. He pitched his first no-hitter at the age of 39, and followed that up the following year by pitching another one at age 40. Spahn also hit nine of his 35 home runs after the age 40, including four in 1961 at the age of 40.

BECOMING A GIANT

After going 4-12 in 20 starts with the lowly Mets, who wound up losing 112 games in 1965, the Mets put Spahn on waivers on July 17, 1965. He immediately signed with the Giants who were battling the rival Dodgers for the National League pennant, with the hope that Spahn would give them an added edge, and perhaps give the lefty one last chance at winning his second World Series title.

Spahn would go 3-4 in 16 starts for San Francisco, who would finish two games behind the league champion Dodgers. That season would be his last for the 44 year-old, as the Giants would release him on October 15, 1965. He would retire soon after.

## Willie Mays – New York Mets

**CAREER HIGHLIGHTS**

- Hall of Fame
- Rookie of the Year
- 2x MVP
- 4x Home Run leader
- 12x Gold Glove winner
- 24x All-Star

During his 21 years as a Giant, Willie Howard Mays was the Rookie-of-the-Year, a two-time league MVP, four-time home run champion, 12-time Gold Glove winner, a batting champion and a 24-time All-Star. He would be part of a 1954 team that would knock off the powerful and highly favored Cleveland Indians in the World Series.

In 1969, Mays would become the second player in MLB history to reach the 600 home run total, and finish with 660 in his career. A year later he would collect his 3,000th hit and finish with 3,293 when he retired in 1973. As of 2022, Mays is still the all-time Giants leader in games played, hits, runs scored, home runs, doubles and total bases; and is second in RBIs.

**BECOMING A MET**

In early May 1972, Giants president Horace C. Stoneham stated that his team needed pitching, and with his aging Mays struggling at the plate and still making $165,000 a year, just below Carl Yastrzemski's Major League leading $167,000, Mays became available when the New York Mets expressed interest. So, on May 11, 1972, after 22 seasons with the Giants, the "Say Hey Kid" was traded to the Mets for Charlie Williams and $50,000.

In 1973, the Mets would capture the NL East title and beat the favored Cincinnati Reds to advance to the World Series, Mays' first since 1962. Mays would go 3-for-10 in four post-season games against the Reds and A's, driving in two runs and scoring two.

## Yogi Berra – New York Mets

**C****AREER** **H****IGHLIGHTS**

- Hall of Fame
- 3x MVP
- 16x All-Star
- 10x World Series winner

At five-foot-seven-and-a-half inches tall, Lawrence Peter "Yogi" Berra won three MVP awards (1951, 1954 and 1955) and hit 30 home runs twice, historically rare feats for a catcher at that time. Berra would drive in over 100 runs five times during his career, and was on the All-Star team in 16 of his 19 major league seasons. He started behind the plate for the American League 11 times.

Berra finished with a career batting average of .285, 358 home runs (306 as a catcher) and 1,430 RBIs. At the time of his retirement, his 306 homers were the most ever as a catcher. He still holds several World Series records, including the most games played (75) and titles (10).

**B****ECOMING A** **M****ET**

Across town, the New York Mets had just finished their third season of play with two former Yankees running the team, general manager George Weiss and manager Casey Stengel. In 1965, Berra accepted an offer from Weiss and joined Stengel's staff as a player-coach. He played in only four games, catching two, and batted .222, playing his final game three days before his 40th birthday in May.

He remained a Mets coach until 1972, when he took over as the club's manager upon the sudden death of Gil Hodges. After finishing in third place that year, he led the team on a remarkable run in 1973, guiding the Mets to the World Series against the Oakland A's.

# National Football League

## Alan Page – Chicago Bears

**CAREER HIGHLIGHTS**

- Hall of Fame
- 9x Pro Bowl
- 1x MVP
- 10+ sacks 6x
- All 1970's Team

As a member of the renowned Minnesota Vikings "Purple People Eater" defense of the 1960's and 70's, Alan Cedric Page became the first defensive player to win the NFL MVP award in 1971. Only Lawrence Taylor has accomplished that since.

Remarkably, Page never missed a game in his entire career, playing in 218 consecutive contests as a defensive tackle (215 as a starter) during which he recovered 22 fumbles, scored three touchdowns (two on fumble recoveries and one on an interception return). He also recorded three safeties, the second most in NFL history, and blocked 23 kicks. He set a career-high with 18 sacks in 1976, and his 148 ½ career sacks were the second most in NFL history when he retired in 1981 (behind Deacon Jones), and is still ranked eighth. He is also one of 11 Vikings to have played in all four of their Super Bowl games.

### BECOMING A BEAR

After excelling in Minnesota for 11 seasons, the 33 year-old Page was waived six games into the 1978 campaign by the Vikings. The Chicago Bears quickly signed him and he moved into the starting lineup without missing a game. Page wound up his career in 1981 after playing 238 games in Chicago, all but three of them as a starter. He would collect 40 sacks during that time, including 11 ½ in the 10 games he played for the Bears in 1978, and 10 in 1979.

## Carl Eller – Seattle Seahawks

**CAREER HIGHLIGHTS**

- Hall of Fame
- 6x Pro Bowl
- All 1970's Team
- 10+ sacks 7x
- 15+ sacks 2x

In 1964, Carl Lee Eller was selected in the first round of the NFL draft by the Minnesota Vikings. He was also selected in the first round of the AFL draft by the Buffalo Bills, who could not sign him. Eller would become the left defensive end in the Vikings front four for the next 15 years and a major contributor as a member of the "Purple People Eaters". Eller was one of 11 Vikings to play in all four of their Super Bowls.

Eller was first-team All-NFL from 1968 to 1971, and again in 1973. He was also second-team All-Pro in 1967 and 1972 and was All-NFC by AP and The Sporting News in 1975. Eller had a nine-year consecutive streak of post-season honors, beginning with his second-team All-pro selection in 1967, and ending with an All-NFC honor in 1975.

**BECOMING A SEAHAWK**

Following the 1978 season, after which he started a career low seven games, the 36-year old Eller was traded with an eighth-round pick to the Seattle Seahawks for defensive tackle Steve Niehaus. Eller played his final season in 1979 with the Seahawks, playing in all 16 games, starting eight, and accumulating three sacks. In his career, Eller only missed three games and started 209 out of the 225 he played.

## Deacon Jones – Washington Redskins

CAREER HIGHLIGHTS

- Hall of Fame
- 8x Pro Bowl
- All 1960's Team
- 10+ sacks 8x
- 20+ sacks 3x

David "Deacon" Jones was selected in the 14th round of the 1961 NFL Draft by the Los Angeles Rams. He soon earned a starting role as a defensive end and teamed with tackle Merlin Olsen to give Los Angeles a perennial All-Pro left side of the defensive line for 11 years as part of the Fearsome Foursome defensive line, considered one of the best units of all time.

Jones won consensus All-Pro honors five straight years from 1965 through 1969 and was second-team All-Pro in 1964, 1970, and 1972. He was also in seven straight Pro Bowls, from 1964 to 1970. In 1964, Jones had 22 sacks in only 14 games. In 1967, Jones had 21.5 sacks, and again tallied 22 sacks in 14 games the following year. His career total of 173.5 sacks was the most by a player at his retirement in 1974, and is currently the third highest total in history.

On January 29, 1972, the 33-year old Jones was traded to the San Diego Chargers for Jeff Staggs and two draft picks. He was named San Diego's defensive captain and led all Chargers' defensive linemen in tackles and won a berth on the AFC Pro Bowl squad.

### BECOMING A REDSKIN

In 1974, Jones signed as a free-agent with the Washington Redskins and was reunited with George Allen, his Rams coach of five years, as a third down rush specialist during which he collected three sacks. In the final game of his NFL career, the Redskins allowed him to kick the point-after-touchdown for the game's last score.

## Don Maynard – Los Angeles Rams

Career Highlights

- Hall of Fame
- 4x Pro Bowl
- 1x TD leader
- 1x receiving yards leader

Donald Rogers Maynard was one of only 20 players who played in the AFL for the league's entire 10-year existence, and one of only seven players who spent their entire AFL careers with one team. Maynard finished his career with 633 receptions for 11,834 yards and 88 touchdowns. His 18.7 yards per catch is the highest for anyone with at least 600 receptions. Maynard was the first receiver to reach 10,000 yards and retired in 1974 as pro football's all-time leader in receptions and yards receiving. Charley Taylor passed him in career receptions in 1975, while Maynard's yardage mark stood until 1986 when Charlie Joiner surpassed him.

Long-standing tensions between Maynard and Jets' Coach Weeb Ewbank boiled over in 1973. After reporting late to Jets' camp that summer, Ewbank traded him to the St. Louis Cardinals for a future draft pick on September 10. Maynard appeared in the first two games under coach Don Coryell and caught one pass for 18 yards, but didn't play in the club's next two contests and was released October 10.

Becoming a Ram

On December 12, just over two months after being released by the Cardinals, the 38 year-old Maynard signed with the playoff-bound Los Angeles Rams, but wasn't activated for their final regular season game, nor their playoff loss to the Dallas Cowboys. Maynard would hook up with the Houston Texans of the World Football League in 1975, but retired after the season after only catching five passes.

## Earl Campbell – New Orleans Saints

CAREER HIGHLIGHTS

- Hall of Fame
- 1x MVP
- 5x Pro Bowl
- 3x Rushing leader
- 5x 1,000 rusher
- 1x Touchdown leader

Earl Christian Campbell was the first player taken in the 1978 NFL Draft by the Houston Oilers after earning All-Southwest Conference honors four years, a consensus All-American and the Heisman Trophy winner in 1977 at the university of Texas. In his nine-season career, Campbell rushed 2,187 times for 9,407 yards, and 74 touchdowns. He would break the 1,000 yard barrier five times, including his first three seasons when he rushed for 1,450, 1,697 and a career high 1,934 yards while scoring 45 touchdowns during that time.

BECOMING A SAINT

In 1984, under new head coach Hugh Campbell, Houston started the season with six straight losses. After rushing for 278 yards in the first six games, Campbell was traded to the New Orleans Saints for their 1985 first round pick, reuniting him with Bum Phillips.

With Campbell and former first round pick and rushing champion George Rogers, the Saints now had two Heisman Trophy winners in the backfield. In his first game with New Orleans, Campbell carried five times for 19 yards, and finished the season with a total of 468 yards and four touchdowns.

Campbell's final 100-yard game was his only one in 1985: a 160-yard outburst against the Minnesota Vikings in which he scored his only touchdown of the season. Campbell finished the year with 643 rushing yards on 158 carries before retiring at the end of the season at the age of 30.

## Emmitt Smith – Arizona Cardinals

CAREER HIGHLIGHTS

- Hall of Fame
- 1x MVP
- 8x Pro Bowl
- 4x Rushing leader
- 11x 1,000 rusher
- 3x Touchdown leader

Emmitt James Smith III is the current NFL leader in career rushing yards with 18,355, breaking the previous record held by Walter Payton. He also leads all running backs with 4,409 rushing attempts, 164 career rushing touchdowns, and his 175 total touchdowns ranks him second only to Jerry Rice's 208. His 21,564 total rushing and receiving yards makes him one of only four players in NFL history to eclipse the 21,000 combined-yards mark, joining Jerry Rice, Brian Mitchell, and Walter Payton.

After 13 years with the Dallas Cowboys, new head coach Bill Parcells decided to go with younger running backs and released the 33-year old Smith on February 26, 2003.

BECOMING A CARDINAL

On March 26, 2003, Smith signed a two-year contract with the Arizona Cardinals who were looking to upgrade their running game and increase their attendance. He finished the 2003 season with 256 rushing yards on 90 carries, missing six games after breaking his shoulder blade, ironically against Dallas on October 5.

In 2004, Smith rebounded with 937 rushing yards and nine touchdowns. Overall in two years with Arizona, Smith had 1,193 rushing yards, 11 rushing touchdowns, and averaged 3.2 yards per carry. Smith technically retired as a Dallas Cowboy after signing a one day contract in 2005 to end his career with the team.

## Franco Harris – Seattle Seahawks

CAREER HIGHLIGHTS

- Hall of Fame
- Rookie of the Year
- 9x Pro Bowl
- 8x 1,000 rusher
- 4x Super Bowl titles

Franco Dok Harris was selected 13th overall in the first round of the 1972 NFL Draft by the Pittsburgh Steelers. As a rookie, he gained 1,055 yards on 188 carries, with an impressive 5.6 yards per carry average. Harris was chosen for nine consecutive Pro Bowls starting his rookie year, and was All-Pro in 1977. Harris rushed for more than 1,000 yards in eight seasons, breaking a record set by Jim Brown. Harris is particularly known for his game winning "Immaculate Reception" during a 1972 playoff game against the Oakland Raiders.

In his 13 professional seasons, Harris gained 12,120 yards on 2,949 carries, a 4.1 yards per carry average, and scored 91 rushing touchdowns. He caught 307 passes for 2,287 yards, a 7.4 yards per reception average, and nine receiving touchdowns.

### BECOMING A SEAHAWK

Following the 1983 season, with Harris and Walter Payton both closing in on Jim Brown's NFL career rushing record, and having just rushed for 1,007 yards that year, Harris asked Steelers management for a pay raise. Believing that Harris was on the downside of his career, however, they refused and Harris threatened to hold out. Instead, the Steelers released him during training camp in 1984 after which he signed with the Seattle Seahawks for the 1984 season. Harris would play just eight games with the team, gaining only 170 yards before retiring at the age of 34, just 192 yards short of Jim Brown's record.

## Jerry Rice – Denver Broncos

CAREER HIGHLIGHTS

- Hall of Fame
- Rookie of the Year
- 13x Pro Bowl
- 6x Reception yard leader
- 4x 100+ reception seasons
- 14x 1,000+ yard seasons
- 11 straight 1,000+ seasons
- 3x Super Bowl titles

Drafted as the 14th pick in the 1st round of the 1985 NFL draft by the San Francisco 49ers, Jerry Lee Rice went on to capture numerous NFL career receiving records, and by a wide margin. His 197 career touchdown receptions are 41 more than second place Randy Moss; his 208 total touchdowns are 33 ahead of runner up Emmitt Smith; and his 22,895 career receiving yards are 5,403 yards ahead of second-place Larry Fitzgerald. His 1,256 career points scored make him the highest-scoring non-kicker in NFL history.

Rice was named to 11 straight pro bowls with the 49ers, and at age 40, caught 92 balls for 1,211 yards with the Oakland Raiders. The NFL honored him as a member of both the NFL 1980s and NFL 1990s All-Decade Team, as well as both the NFL 75th Anniversary All-Time Team and 100th Anniversary All-Time Team.

BECOMING A BRONCO

After two years with the Oakland Raiders and one with the Seattle Seahawks, Rice signed a one-year, $790,000 contract with the Denver Broncos prior to the 2004 season. Although he participated in training camp, Rice was cut during camp, thus never played a regular season game for the Broncos. Ironically, the last catch he ever made was in a preseason game for Denver against the 49ers, where he caught one ball for eight yards. Like Emmitt Smith with the Cowboys, Rice signed a one-day contract with San Francisco in 2005 in order to retire as a 49er.

## Joe Montana – Kansas City Chiefs

**Career Highlights**

- Hall of Fame
- 2x MVP
- 8x Pro Bowls
- 4x Super Bowl titles
- 2x Passing leader
- 4x Completion % leader

In the 1979 NFL draft, the San Francisco 49ers selected Joseph Clifford Montana Jr at the end of the third round with the 82nd overall pick. Montana was the fourth quarterback taken, behind Jack Thompson, Phil Simms, and Steve Fuller, all selected in the first round.

During his time with the 49ers, Montana completed 2,929 of 4,600 passes for 35,142 yards with 244 touchdowns and 123 interceptions. He had thirty-five 300-yard passing games including seven in which he threw for over 400 yards. For his career, he had 3,409 completions on 5,391 attempts, 273 touchdowns, 139 interceptions, and 40,551 yards passing. When Montana retired, his career passer rating was 92.3, second only to his 49er successor Steve Young's 96.8. His overall record as a starter was 117–47.

### BECOMING A CHIEF

After Steve Young supplanted him as the starting quarterback in San Francisco following two injury-riddled seasons, Montana requested a trade and was dealt to the Kansas City Chiefs on April 20, 1993, signing a $10 million contract over three years. His trade was the catalyst for the Chiefs' free-agent signing of star Los Angeles Raiders running back Marcus Allen on June 9. Together, the former Super Bowl MVPs lead the Chiefs to their first division title in 22 years in 1993. Kansas City would make the playoffs again in 1994, but were eliminated both years. On April 18, 1995, the 38 year-old Montana announced his retirement at Justin Herman Plaza in San Francisco.

## Joe Namath – Los Angeles Rams

CAREER HIGHLIGHTS

- Hall of Fame
- Rookie of the Year
- AFL Player of the Year
- 5x Pro Bowls
- 3x Passing yardage leader

Joe William Namath played college football for the Alabama Crimson Tide, where he won the national championship as a senior, and was selected by the Jets first overall in the 1965 AFL draft.

During his five AFL seasons, Namath was named player of the year in 1968 and twice led the league in passing yards, while winning one AFL championship and one Super Bowl. Both victories remain the Jets' only championships. In 1967, he was the first quarterback to throw more than 4,000 yards in a season. Following the 1970 AFL–NFL merger, he was the league's passing yards and touchdowns leader during the 1972 season. He played in New York for four more seasons.

### BECOMING A RAM

After twelve years with the Jets, Namath was waived prior to the 1977 season to facilitate a move to the Los Angeles Rams when a trade could not be worked out. Hoping to revive his career, knee injuries, a bad hamstring, and a decade as an NFL quarterback had taken their toll on the 34 year-old. After a 2–1 start, Namath took a beating on a cold and rainy Monday Night Football game against the Chicago Bears, throwing four interceptions. He was benched as a starter for the rest of the season after playing in four games, and announced his retirement in January, 1978.

## Johnny Unitas – San Diego Chargers

**CAREER HIGHLIGHTS**

- Hall of Fame
- 3x MVP
- 10x Pro Bowls
- 4x Passing leader
- All 1960's team

John Constatine Unitas was drafted by the Pittsburgh Steelers in the ninth round of the 1955 draft, but was released before the season began as the odd man out among four quarterbacks trying to fill three spots. He joined the Baltimore Colts in 1956, where he played the next 16 years. Unitas finished his 18 NFL seasons with 2,830 completions in 5,186 attempts for 40,239 yards and 290 touchdown, the most of any quarterback at the time of his retirement, despite being plagued by arm trouble in the latter part of his career. Unitas was the first quarterback to throw for more than 40,000 yards, despite playing during an era when NFL teams played shorter seasons of 12 or 14 games. His 32 touchdown passes in 1959 and 47-game consecutive touchdown streak between 1956 and 1960 were records at the time.

### BECOMING A CHARGER

After being benched in the latter half of the 1972 season, Unitas was traded from the Colts to the San Diego Chargers on January 20, 1973, and signed a two-year deal on June 8. He succeeded long time Charger quarterback John Hadl, who had been traded to the Los Angeles Rams.

Unitas started the 1973 season with a 38–0 loss to the Washington Redskins, throwing for just 55 yards with three interceptions and was sacked eight times. His final victory as a starter came against the Buffalo Bills in week 2 where Unitas went 10–18 for 175 yards and two touchdown passes in a 34–7 rout. Two weeks later against the Pittsburgh Steelers, he threw two first-half interceptions, going 2-for-9 for 19 yards before being replaced by rookie quarterback Dan Fouts. After a 1–3 record as a starter, Unitas retired in the preseason of 1974.

## Ken Stabler – New Orleans Saints

CAREER HIGHLIGHTS

- Hall of Fame
- 1x MVP
- 4x Pro Bowls
- 2x Passing leader
- All 1970's team

Before being selected in the second round of the 1968 draft by the Oakland Raiders, Kenneth Michael Stabler succeeded Joe Namath at Alabama and led the Crimson Tide to a national championship in 1965, was a first-team All-American (1967), and first-team All-SEC (1967). After choosing professional football over Major League Baseball (he had been drafted by the Yankees, Mets and Astros), Stabler would play the next 11 years with the Raiders, and another five with the Houston Oilers and New Orleans Saints.

When he retired in 1985, his 60% completion percentage was the second highest in NFL history behind Joe Montana of the San Francisco 49ers. His 27,938 yards were 11th all-time, and his 194 touchdowns 13th all-time. Stabler's five consecutive appearances in conference championship games (from 1973-1977) remained a record for NFL quarterbacks until Tom Brady passed him in 2016.

BECOMING A SAINT

After subpar 1978 and 1979 seasons in which the Raiders failed to make the playoffs, Stabler was traded in March 1980 to the Oilers for Dan Pastorini. After being released by Houston following the 1981 season, Stabler signed with the New Orleans Saints after starter David Wilson went down with a season ending knee injury. Stabler would start 22 of 25 games as a Saint and complete 56.6% of his passes. In February 1984, the Saints acquired New York Jets quarterback Richard Todd. After playing in just two games, both off the bench, Stabler and his bad knees would decide to retire in October 1984 at the age of 39.

## Lance Alworth – Dallas Cowboys

CAREER HIGHLIGHTS

- Hall of Fame
- 7x Pro Bowl
- 3x Reception leader
- 3x Reception yards leader
- All 1960's team

Lance Dwight Alworth was chosen as the eight overall pick in the first round of the 1962 NFL draft by the San Francisco 49ers. The AFL's Oakland Raiders selected him with their ninth pick in the second round of the 1962 AFL Draft, and then traded his rights to the San Diego Chargers in return for halfback Bo Roberson, quarterback Hunter Enis, and offensive tackle Gene Selawski. Alworth opted to sign with the Chargers instead of the 49ers.

A rare mistake by the Raiders, as from 1964–1969, Alworth led the league in receptions, receiving yards, receiving touchdowns, and total touchdowns three times each. He set a record of seven consecutive seasons with over 1,000 receiving yards that lasted 30 years until broken by Jerry Rice with 11, and was the first player with back-to-back seasons averaging 100+ receiving yards per game. Alworth still shares the record for the most regular-season games with 200+ receiving yards with five.

### BECOMING A COWBOY

Alworth's productivity sharply declined in 1970, snagging 35 catches for 608 yards, and on May 19, 1971 was traded to the Dallas Cowboys for Tony Liscio, Pettis Norman, and Ron East where he would play his final two seasons.

In Super Bowl VI following the 1971 season, he scored the game's first touchdown, a 7-yard touchdown pass from Roger Staubach in the Cowboys' 24-3 victory over the Miami Dolphins. Alworth retired after the 1972 season at age 32.

## Randy Moss – San Francisco 49ers

CAREER HIGHLIGHTS

- Hall of Fame
- Rookie of the Year
- 6x Pro Bowl
- 5x Receiving TD leader
- All 2000's team

Randy Gene Moss played in the NFL for 14 seasons with the Minnesota Vikings, Oakland Raiders, New England Patriots, Tennessee Titans and the San Francisco 49ers. Moss holds the NFL single-season touchdown reception record with 23 in 2007, as well as the NFL single-season touchdown reception record for a rookie with 17 in 1998. Moss led the league in touchdown receptions five times, and ranks second in career touchdown (156) as well as fourth in career receiving yards (15,292).

Thirty-three year old Moss finished the 2010 season with the Tennessee Titans, collecting career lows in receptions (28) and receiving yards (393). The Titans stated that they did not plan to re-sign Moss for the 2011 season, and he became a free agent. On August 1, 2011, Moss decided to retire from professional football.

BECOMING A 49ER

On February 13, 2012, his 35th birthday, Moss announced that he was coming out of retirement and was ready to play again. On March 12, Moss signed a one-year contract with the 49ers after a workout with the team's head coach Jim Harbaugh. On September 9, 2012, Moss caught his 154th touchdown reception, and subsequently passed Terrell Owens for sole possession of second on the all-time receiving touchdown list. Moss went on to play in Super Bowl XLVII that year, where he had two receptions for 41 yards in a 34–31 loss to the Baltimore Ravens.

## Reggie White – Carolina Panthers

**CAREER HIGHLIGHTS**

- Hall of Fame
- 2x MVP
- 13x Pro Bowl
- 2x Sack leader
- #2 All-time sack leader
- All 1980's team
- All 1990's team

Reginald Howard White was a two-time NFL Defensive Player of the Year, Super Bowl XXXI champion, and a 13-time Pro Bowl and All-Pro selection. He's second all-time among NFL career sack leaders with 198 behind Bruce Smith's 200. White was selected to the NFL 75th and 100th Anniversary All-Time Teams, and the NFL 1980s and 1990s All-Decade Teams. During his professional career, he was also known for his Christian ministry as an ordained evangelical minister, leading to his nickname, "the Minister of Defense".

Out of college, White joined the USFL Memphis Showboats before signing with the Philadelphia Eagles after the league folded. After eight seasons in Philadelphia and six in Green Bay, White initially decided to retire following the 1998 season after winning his second NFL Defensive Player of the Year award while collecting 16 sacks at the age of 37.

### BECOMING A PANTHER

In 2000, White came out of a one-year retirement and started all 16 games for the Carolina Panthers. He had five and a half sacks and one forced fumble while with the team. He again retired at the end of the 2000 season. Four years later, White would sadly die of cardiac and pulmonary sarcoidosis, a condition that he had lived with for years.

## Ronnie Lott – Kansas City Chiefs



CAREER HIGHLIGHTS

- Hall of Fame
- 2x MVP
- 10x Pro Bowl
- 2x Interception leader
- 4x Super Bowl titles
- All 1980's team
- All 1990's team

Ronald Mandel Lott was drafted by the San Francisco 49ers with the eighth pick in the first round of the 1981 draft, initially as a cornerback. In his 14 NFL seasons, most as a safety, Lott recorded 63 interceptions, fourth best all-time at his retirement, which he returned for 730 yards and five touchdowns. He recovered 17 fumbles, returning them for 43 yards. Lott also played in 20 postseason games, recording nine interceptions, 89 tackles, one forced fumble, one fumble recovery, and scoring two touchdowns. Additionally, he was named All-Pro eight times, All-NFC six times, and All-AFC once. Lott was also named to the NFL's 75th Anniversary Team in 1994 and the 100th Anniversary Team in 2019.

After his career with San Francisco, Lott signed as a free agent in 1991 with the Los Angeles Raiders, where he lead the league in interceptions for the second time with eight. In 1993, Lott signed with the New York Jets, which would be the last team he would play a regular season game with.

BECOMING A CHIEF

In 1995, Lott signed with the Kansas City Chiefs, but was injured in the preseason and never played for them. He would contemplate rejoining the 49ers later in 1995, but the injuries he had suffered in recent years forced him to retire at age 35 instead.

# Tim Brown – Tampa Bay Buccaneers

CAREER HIGHLIGHTS

- Hall of Fame
- 9x Pro Bowl
- 1x Reception leader
- All 1990's team

When Timothy Donell Brown retired in 2005, he had collected 14,934 receiving yards, the second-highest total in NFL history, 1,094 receptions (3rd), and 100 touchdown catches (3rd). Brown also gained 190 rushing yards, 3,320 punt-return yards (5th in NFL history), and 1,235 yards returning kickoffs. His 19,682 combined net yards ranked him #5 all-time when he retired. He also scored 105 total touchdowns in four different ways (100 receiving, 1 rushing, 3 punt returns, 1 kickoff return).

Not wanting to accept a smaller role, the Oakland Raiders released Brown on August 5, 2004 after 16 years with the team, a move that did not go over well with Raider fans or his Raider teammates. He was also the last of the Los Angeles Raiders to play in Oakland.

## BECOMING AN BUCCANEER

Five days after his release, Brown signed with the Tampa Bay Buccaneers and former Raider head coach Jon Gruden. In his single season in Tampa, Brown caught 24 passes for 200 yards and one touchdown in 15 games. During his time with the Bucs, Brown reached 100 career receiving touchdowns, tying him with Steve Largent for 3rd on the NFL's all-time career receiving touchdown list at that time behind former teammate Jerry Rice (197) and Cris Carter (130).

In July 2005, Brown signed a one-day contract with the Raiders to retire with the team.

## Tony Dorsett – Denver Broncos

Career Highlights

- Hall of Fame
- Rookie of the Year
- 1x MVP
- 4x Pro Bowl
- 8x 1,000+ seasons

Anthony Drew Dorsett Sr. rushed for 12,739 yards and 77 touchdowns during his 12-year career. On January 3, 1983, during a Monday Night Football game in Minnesota, Dorsett broke a 99-yard touchdown run against the Vikings, the longest run from scrimmage in NFL history at the time.

Dorsett made the Pro Bowl four times during his career, and rushed for over 1,000 yards in eight of his first nine seasons.

With the drafting of 24-year old Hershal Walker in 1986, the 34-year old Dorsett saw his playing time dwindle, with Walker also not happy at sharing time in the backfield. In 1987, Dorsett demanded a trade after not playing in two games despite being healthy.

Becoming a Bronco

On June 2, 1988, Dorsett was traded to the Denver Broncos in exchange for a conditional fifth-round draft choice and reunited with former Cowboys offensive coordinator Dan Reeves. Dorsett led the team that season with 703 rushing yards and five rushing touchdowns. On September 26, 1988, Dorsett moved into second place on the all-time rushing list with 12,306 yards, and finished his career with 12,739 yards, trailing only Walter Payton.

He retired at age 34 after having torn left knee ligaments during training camp in 1989.

# National Basketball Association

## Bob Cousy – Cincinnati Royals

CAREER HIGHLIGHTS

- Hall of Fame
- 1x MVP
- 13x All-Star
- 8x Assist champ
- 6x NBA titles
- NBA 75th Anniversary team

Robert Joseph Cousy was a core piece during the early half of the Boston Celtics dynasty, winning six NBA championships during his 13-year tenure with the team, while being named an All-Star each year. Nicknamed "The Houdini of the Hardwood", Cousy was the NBA assists leader for eight consecutive seasons, and was regarded as the first great point guard of the NBA. He was the first to reach the 4,000, 5,000, and 6,000 career assists milestones.

Cousy concluded his career in Boston with three consecutive NBA titles before retiring after the third one in 1962-63 against the Los Angeles Lakers at the age of 34. In 917 regular season games as a Celtic, Cousy would average 18.5 points and 7.6 assists a game. In 109 playoff games, he also averaged 18.5 points a game, while passing out 8.6 assists per contest.

BECOMING A ROYAL

After retiring from the Celtics, Cousy became the head coach of Boston College until 1969, going 114-38 during his time there. Missing professional basketball, Cousy returned to the NBA as coach of the Cincinnati Royals later that year. Late in the 1969-70 season, Cousy, at age 41, made a late-season comeback as a player for seven games, averaging 0.7 points and 1.4 assists per game. He continued as the Royals coach until early in the 1973–74 NBA season when he stepped down with a 141–209 record.

## Dominique Wilkins – Orlando Magic

**Career Highlights**

- Hall of Fame
- 9x All-Star
- 1x Scoring champ
- NBA 75th Anniversary team

Jacques Dominique Wilkins was the third pick in the 1982 draft, originally selected by the Utah Jazz. After refusing to play power forward for the cash-strapped team, he was traded to the Atlanta Hawks.

During his career, Wilkins averaged more than 25 points per game for ten consecutive seasons, and captured a scoring title in 1985–86 with an average of 30.3 points per game. Wilkins was instrumental in the Hawks' record four consecutive 50-win seasons during the 1980s. A nine-time NBA All-Star and the winner of two NBA slam dunk contests, Wilkins registered 26,668 points and 7,169 rebounds in his NBA career. He ranked in the top 10 on the NBA scoring list at the time of his retirement, and  number 17 in 2024.

After 12 seasons with the Hawks, Wilkins played single seasons with the Los Angeles Clippers, Boston Celtics and San Antonio Spurs. After one season with the Spurs, Wilkins went overseas to play for  Fortitudo Bologna of the Italian League for the 1997–98 season.

### Becoming a Magic

In February 1999, Wilkins returned to play his last season in the NBA with the Orlando Magic, alongside his brother Gerald Wilkins. In 27 games, he averaged 5.0 points and 2.6 rebounds per game. Wilkins was waived after the season and retired at the age of 39.

# George Gervin – Chicago Bulls

CAREER HIGHLIGHTS

- Hall of Fame
- 12x All-Star
- 4x Scoring champ
- 2x All ABA
- ABA All-Time team
- NBA 75th Anniversary team

After playing for Eastern Michigan University and the Pontiac Chaparrals of the Continental Basketball Association, George "the Iceman" Gervin signed a contract to play with the Virginia Squires of the ABA in January 1973. A year later he was sold to the San Antonio Spurs, and continued to play for them after the team merged into the NBA in 1976.

In his 12 seasons with the Spurs, Gervin averaged over 26 points a game, leading the NBA in scoring four times. When he retired, Gervin had averaged 25.1 points, 5.3 rebounds, and 2.6 assists per game, with a field goal percentage of 50.4%. His 26,595 combined NBA/ABA points ranks him 18th all-time.

## BECOMING AN BULL

Right before the 1985–86 season began, the Spurs traded the 33-year old Gervin to the Chicago Bulls after he missed preseason workouts and with the growing possibility of him being relegated to the bench. He would play in all 82 games for the Bulls, averaging 16.2 points a game, including a season-high 45 points against the Dallas Mavericks, but would retire from the NBA at the end of the season.

His basketball career didn't end, however, as Gervin would play in Italy during the 1986-87 season and average 26.1 points a game. After playing one year with the Quad City Thunder of the Continental Basketball Association, Gervin would return to Europe and play one season in Spain for TDK Manresa, where he would average 25.1 points a game at the age of 38 before retiring for good.

## Hakeem Olajuwon – Toronto Raptors

CAREER HIGHLIGHTS

- Hall of Fame
- 1x MVP
- 12x All-Star
- 9x All Defense
- 2x Rebound leader
- NBA 75th Anniversary team

Hazeem Abdul Olajuwon was the number one pick in the 1984 NBA draft after the Houston Rockets won a coin toss over the Portland Trailblazers. Olajuwon, a player for the University of Houston, entered the NBA draft early in the hopes that the Rockets would win the coin toss. They did, and the Trailblazers took center Sam Bowie as the second pick.

In 1994, Olajuwon helped lead the Rockets to their first ever NBA championship, and the city of Houston's first title since 1961 when the Oilers won the AFL championship, after they defeated the New York Knicks in seven games. That year he became the only player in NBA history to win the MVP, the NBA Championship, the Finals MVP and Defensive Player of the Year awards in the same season.

For his NBA career, Olajuwon averaged 21.8 points on 51% shooting, 11.1 rebounds, 2.5 assists, and 3.1 blocks per game in 1,238 career contests.

### BECOMING AN RAPTOR

After refusing a $13 million deal with the Rockets, the 38 year-old Olajuwon was traded to the Toronto Raptors in August, 2001 for draft picks. In his first game with the Raptors, he scored 11 points in just 22 minutes of playing time against the Orlando Magic. Olajuwon averaged career lows of 7.1 points and 6.0 rebounds per game in the 61 games he played that season in what would be his final one in the NBA, as he decided to retire in the fall of 2002 due to a back injury.

## Karl Malone – Los Angeles Lakers

**CAREER HIGHLIGHTS**

- Hall of Fame
- 2x MVP
- 14x All-Star
- 4x All Defense
- 2x Rebound leader
- NBA 75th Anniversary team

Karl Anthony Malone spent 19 seasons in the NBA, 18 with the Utah Jazz, and formed a formidable duo with teammate guard John Stockton. In December 1989, "the Mailman" recorded 52 points and 17 rebounds in a road win over the Charlotte Hornets. A month later he scored a career-high 61 points against the Milwaukee Bucks when he made 21 of 26 field goals and 19 of 23 free throws

Over 1,476 NBA games and 1,471 starts (never coming off the bench after his rookie season), Malone scored 36,928 points, third best all-time, for an average of 25.0 per game on 51.6% shooting. Malone also snagged 10.1 rebounds and 1.41 steals per game for his career.

### BECOMING A LAKER

Malone signed as a free agent with the Los Angeles Lakers after the 2002-03 season at age 40, joining fellow free agent Gary Payton and Laker stars Kobe Bryan and Shaquille O'Neal to form a super team in an attempt to win his first NBA championship. Malone would miss 39 regular season games with a knee injury, and average 13.2 points and 8.7 rebounds per game in 42 contests.

In the playoffs, the Lakers would advance to the NBA championship, but lose to the Detroit Pistons in five games. Malone would average 11.5 points and 8.8 rebounds in playoff action with Los Angeles. Despite being recruited by the New York Knicks and San Antonio Spurs in the offseason, Malone decided to retire after 19 seasons.

# Michael Jordan – Washington Wizards

CAREER HIGHLIGHTS

- Hall of Fame
- 5x MVP
- 14x All-Star
- 9x All Defense
- 10x Scoring Leader
- NBA 75th Anniversary team

Michael Jeffrey "Air" Jordan's impressive individual accomplishments include six NBA Finals MVP awards, 10 NBA scoring titles, five NBA MVP awards, nine All-Defensive First Team honors, 14 NBA All-Star Game selections, three NBA steals titles, and the 1988 NBA Defensive Player of the Year Award. He holds the NBA records for career regular season scoring average (30.1 points per game) and career playoff scoring average (33.4 points per game).

In his third season, Jordan led the NBA in scoring with 37.1 points a game while averaging 40 minutes. Three years later, on March 28, 1990, Jordan scored a career-high 69 points in a 117–113 road win over the Cleveland Cavaliers.

Following the murder of his father, Jordan abruptly retired from basketball before the 1993–94 NBA season to play Minor League Baseball in the Chicago White Sox organization, but returned to the Bulls in March 1995 and led them to three championships. He retired for the second and final time.

BECOMING A WIZARD

On September 25, 2001, Jordan announced his return to the NBA to play for the Washington Wizards. In an injury-plagued 2001–02 season, Jordan led the team in scoring (22.9), assists (5.2), and steals (1.4) in 60 games.

After announcing that 2002-03 would be his last season, the 39 year-old Jordan played in all 82 games for Washington, averaging 20 points, 3.8 assists and 1.5 steals per game.

## Nate Thurmond – Cleveland Cavaliers

**CAREER HIGHLIGHTS**

- Hall of Fame
- 7x All-Star
- 5x All Defense
- NBA 75th Anniversary team

As a rookie in 1963, Nathaniel Thurmond played a supporting role alongside center Wilt Chamberlain and averaged 7.0 points and 10.4 rebounds, while being named to the NBA All-Rookie Team in 1964.

After Chamberlain's departure during the 1964-65 season, Thurmond's production increased, and between 1967 and 1972 would average over 20 and over 18 rebounds per game.

On October 18, 1974, in his first game after being traded by the Warriors to the Chicago Bulls, Thurmond recorded 22 points, 14 rebounds, 13 assists and 12 blocked shots against the Atlanta Hawks, becoming the first player in NBA history to officially record a quadruple-double.

Known for his defensive play, Thurmond is one of five players in NBA history to average at least 15 rebounds per game for his career; one of five players to average at least 20 rebounds per game during a season (achieved three times); and one of four players to record 40 or more rebounds in a game. In addition, he holds the NBA regular season record for rebounds in a quarter with 18.

### BECOMING A CAVALIER

Thirteen games into the 1975–76 season, Thurmond was part of a trade made between the Bulls and Cleveland Cavaliers. In Cleveland, Thurmond filled in for injured center Jim Chones to help lead Cleveland to the NBA Eastern Conference finals before losing to the Boston Celtics.

After playing in 49 games and averaging 5.5 points and 7.6 rebounds as a part-time player the following year, the 35 year-old Thurmond retired at the end of the 1976–77 season.

## Patrick Ewing – Orlando Magic

CAREER HIGHLIGHTS

- Hall of Fame
- Rookie of the Year
- 11x All-Star
- 3x All Defense
- NBA 75th Anniversary team

Patrick Aloysius Ewing Sr. was the first pick in the 1985 draft by the New York Knicks in the first year the NBA held a drawing for the #1 pick.

In 1,183 games over 17 seasons, Ewing averaged 21.0 points, 9.8 rebounds, and 2.4 blocks per game, and averaged better than a 50% shooting percentage. During his career, Ewing was top 10 in field goal percentage eight times, top 10 in rebounds per game and total rebounds eight times, top 10 in points and points per game eight times, and top 10 in blocks per game for 13 years.

In 1999, Ewing became the 10th player in NBA history to record 22,000 points and 10,000 rebounds.

Following the 2000 season, after 15 year and over 1,000 games played, Ewing requested a trade from New York. On September 20, 2000 the Knicks complied and sent the 38 year-old Ewing to the Seattle Super Sonics in a four-team trade. In one season with Seattle, Ewing averaged just over nine points and seven rebounds a game in 79 games

BECOMING A MAGIC

In 2001, Ewing signed with the Orlando Magic as a free agent. In 64 games with Orlando, Ewing averaged six points and four rebounds while averaging just 14 minutes a game before retiring at the end of the season at the age of 39.

# Rick Barry – Houston Rockets

**CAREER HIGHLIGHTS**

- Hall of Fame
- 12x All-Star
- 2x Scoring Leader
- 7x Free Throw Leader
- NBA 75th Anniversary team
- ABA all-time team

Richard Francis Dennis Barry III ranks among the greatest all-around players in basketball history. He is the only player to have led the NCAA, ABA, and NBA in scoring in a season. He ranks as the all-time ABA scoring leader in the regular season (30.5 points per game) and postseason (33.5), while his 36.3 points per game are the most in the NBA Finals history. Barry was also the first player to score at least 50 points in a playoff game 7 in either league. He is one of only four players to be a part of a championship team in both the ABA and NBA.

Known for his under hand free throw style, Barry's career .880 free throw percentage ranks first in ABA history, while his .900 percentage was the best of any NBA player at the time of his retirement in 1980.

## BECOMING A ROCKET

In 1978, at the age of 34, Barry was still averaging 23.1 points per game, although his minutes were dropping. With his contract expiring after the season, Barry was looking for one more large payday before calling it a career. The Warriors, however, were in the middle of a youth movement and didn't want to invest big money to one player. And so, in 1979, they reluctantly let him go and Barry signed as a free agent with the Houston Rockets where he played two years, averaging 13.5 and 12.0 points per season. The NBA would later award the Warriors 24-year-old playmaking guard John Lucas from the Rockets as compensation.

## Shaquille O'Neal – Boston Celtics

Career Highlights

- Hall of Fame
- 1x MVP
- 15x All-Star
- 3x All Defense
- 2x Scoring Leader
- NBA 75th Anniversary team

Shaquille Rashaun O'Neal, a two-time All-American center with the LSU Tigers, was drafted by the Orlando Magic with the 1st overall pick in the 1992 NBA draft. The 7-foot-1-inch, 325-pound center played for six teams over his 19-year career and is a four-time NBA champion. "Shaq" is one of only three players to win NBA MVP, All-Star Game MVP and Finals MVP awards in the same year (2000); the other players being Willis Reed in 1970 and Michael Jordan in 1996 and 1998.

O'Neal was the third-ranked player all-time in free throws taken with 11,252 in 1,207 games. On December 25, 2008, O'Neal missed his 5,000th free throw, becoming the second player in NBA history to do so, along with Wilt Chamberlain. O'Neal made one three-point shot in his career, going 1 for 22. Shaq played four seasons in Orlando, eight in Los Angeles, four in Miami, two in Phoenix and one in Cleveland, and ranks eighth all-time in points scored, sixth in field goals, 15th in rebounds, and eighth in blocks as of 2023.

Becoming a Celtic

After losing the NBA championship to the Boston Celtics in 2010, O'Neal left the Cleveland Cavaliers to join the reigning champs, hoping for one more title shot. Injuries would plague the 38 year-old all season, however, limiting Shaq to 37 games, mostly has a backup. His 9.2 points and 4.8 rebounds a game would be career lows. After the Miami Heat eliminated the Celtics in the second round of the playoffs, O'Neal announced his retirement on June 3, 2011.

## Walt Frazier – Cleveland Cavaliers

**CAREER HIGHLIGHTS**

- Hall of Fame
- 7x All-Star
- 7x All Defense
- NBA 75th Anniversary team

Walter "Clyde" Frazier Jr. was drafted fifth overall by the New York Knicks, and averaged 9.0 points per game, earning a berth on the NBA All-Rookie Team in 1967–68. In his second season, Frazier's 17.5 points, 7.9 assists, and 6.2 rebounds per game averages made him one of the most improved players in the league.

"Clyde" helped lead the Knicks to world championships in 1970 and 1973, both over the Los Angeles Laker. In 1976, Frazier was selected for his seventh and final NBA All-Star Game.

Frazier held Knicks franchise records for most games (759), minutes played (28,995), field goals attempted (11,669), field goals made (5,736), free throws attempted (4,017), free throws made (3,145), assists (4,791) and points (14,617) before the arrival of Patrick Ewing, who would break most of his team records. He averaged 19.3 points and 6.3 assists a game during his time as a Knick.

### BECOMING A CAVALIER

On the eve of the 1977-78 season, New York sent Frazier to the Cleveland Cavaliers as compensation for the free-agent signing of younger guard Jim Cleamons, shocking Frazier, and angering many Knick fans who didn't want to see their favorite player leave.

Frazier played only 66 games in three seasons with the Cavaliers. He retired midway through the 1979–80 season at the age of 34 after playing in only three games and averaging 3.3 points and 2.7 assists per contest.

## Wilt Chamberlain – San Diego Conquistadors

CAREER HIGHLIGHTS

- Hall of Fame
- Rookie of the Year
- 4x MVP
- 13x All-Star
- 11x Rebounding Leader
- 7x Scoring Leader
- 1x Assist Leader
- NBA 75th Anniversary team

Although Wilton Norman Chamberlain is best-remembered as the only player to score 100 points in a single game, he also once collected 55 rebounds in a single contest, and is the only player to average 30 points and 20 rebounds per game in a season, a feat he accomplished seven times. In 1961-62 alone, "Wilt the Stilt" averaged 50 points and 48 minutes per game.

Other records held include most games with 50+ points (118); most consecutive games with 40+ points (14); most consecutive games with 30+ points (65); most consecutive games with 20+ points (126); highest rookie scoring average for a season (37.6); and highest field goal percentage in a season (.727). During his 14 year career, Chamberlain averaged 30.1 points and 22.9 rebounds per game.

BECOMING A CONQUISTADOR

In 1973, a contract spat with the Lakers lead Chamberlain to sign with the San Diego Conquistadors, a member of the NBA-rival ABA league, as a player-coach. Due to legal issues with his Laker contract, a judge ruled on opening day of the Conquistadors' 1973-74 season that Chamberlain could coach the Conquistadors but could not play for any team other than the Lakers that year So although Chamberlain never did play a game for the Conquistador's, his career did end with them.

# National Hockey League

## Bobby Hull – Hartford Whalers

CAREER HIGHLIGHTS

- Hall of Fame
- 3x Ross winner
- 2x Hart winner
- 12x All-Star
- 8x Goals leader

In 1961-62, Robert Marvin Hull became the third player in NHL history to score 50 goals in a season. The left wing would do so three more times that decade, scoring 54 in 1965-66, 52 in 1966-67 and 58 in 1968-69. He would score 107 points that year, breaking the 100 point mark for the only time in his NHL career.

In 1972, at the age of 33 and unhappy with his salary, Hull bolted to the upstart World Hockey League (WHL) where he would play for the next seven years with the Winnipeg Jets, leading them to three titles. In 1974-75, Hull set career highs of 77 goals and 142 points and win his second Gordie Howe MVP trophy in three years.

Howe would retire following the 1978 season after the WHL folded. The Winnipeg Jets, however, would be revived in the NHL the following year. Still technically a member of the NHL Chicago Black Hawks, the Jets selected Howe from the Black Hawks in the 1979 NHL expansion draft. Howe would play in 18 games and score 10 points (four goals, six assists) for Winnipeg in 1979-80.

### BECOMING A WHALER

On February 27, 1980, Howe was traded by the Jets to the Hartford Whalers, where he would play in nine games and score seven points (two goals, five assists) the last two months of the season. He would retire at the end of the season at the age of 41.

## Bobby Orr – Chicago Blackhawks

CAREER HIGHLIGHTS

- Hall of Fame
- 2x Ross winner
- 3x Hart winner
- 8x Norris winner
- 2x Smythe winner
- 9x All-Star

Playing 12 seasons in the NHL, the first 10 with the Boston Bruins, Robert Gordon Orr is credited for revolutionizing the position of defenseman, as he is the only defenseman to win the league scoring title with two Art Ross Trophies, while also winning a record eight consecutive Norris Trophies as the NHL's best defenseman and three consecutive Hart Trophies as the league's MVP.

In 1970-71, Orr became the first player to dish out over 100 assists in a single season with 102. Wayne Gretzky joined him eight years later and Mario Lemieux 10 years after that. As of 2024, they are still the only three players to have achieved 100 assists in a season. Orr's 139 points in 1970-71 are still the most ever by a defenseman in an NHL season.

Over a dozen knee surgeries forced Orr to retire following the 1978-79 season at age 30. As a result, he became the youngest player to be inducted into the Hockey Hall of Fame at age 31 in 1979.

### BECOMING A BLACK HAWK

In September 1975, Orr signed a five year guaranteed contract with the Chicago Blackhawks, spurning the reduced five year offer and only one year guaranteed deal from Boston. With his knees not getting any better, the Bruins required that Orr pass a physical each year to get paid. Chicago didn't, so he went with them. Orr and his knees would only last two years with the Blackhawks, playing in 26 games and scoring six goals with 21 assists.

## Chris Chelios – Atlanta Thrashers

CAREER HIGHLIGHTS

- Hall of Fame
- 3x Norris winner
- 16x All-Star
- 3x Cup winner

Christos Konstantinos Chelios played defense for the Montreal Canadians, Chicago Blackhawks, Detroit Red Wings and Atlanta Thrashers during a record-tying 26 year career, sharing the honor with Gordie Howe. Chelios was an All-Star 15 seasons in a row beginning in 1987-88.

During his final season in 2009-10, Chelios was the oldest active player in the NHL at 48 years of age, and the second oldest of all-time. He had played in more games in the NHL by a defenseman until passed by Zdeno Chára in 2021-22. Chelios still holds the record for most career playoff games by any player with 266, as well as the most career penalty minutes for a defenseman with 423.

On May 1, 2009, he appeared in the playoffs for an NHL record 24th time, having missed them only once. In 2017, Chelios was named one of the "100 Greatest NHL Players" in history

### BECOMING A THRASHER

After Detroit announced that they would not be re-signing Chelios for the 2009-10 season, he signed a 25-game contract with the Chicago Wolves of the American Hockey League. After a second 25-game contract with the Wolves, Chelios signed a two-way contract with the Atlanta Thrashers, allowing him to remain with the Wolves until he was recalled to the Thrashers, He would play in seven games for the Thrashers in 2009-10, but failed to record any points. On August 31, 2010, Chelios officially retired at the age of 48.

# Eric Lindros – Dallas Stars

**Career Highlights**

- Hall of Fame
- 1x Pearson winner
- 1x Hart winner
- 2x All-Star

Eric Bryan Lindros was the first pick of the Quebec Nordiques in the 1991 NHL Entry draft, despite notifying the team that he wouldn't play for them. The Nordiques would eventually trade him to the Philadelphia Flyers for a package of players and draft picks.

Lindros would score over 40 goals in each of his first two seasons as a 19 and 20 year old center, and win the Hart Memorial Trophy as MVP in the lockout-shortened 1995 season after scoring 29 goals and 41 assists in 46 games, while leading the Flyers to their first playoff appearance in six years.

Lindros became a restricted free agent following the 1999-2000 season and sat out all of 2000-01 when the Flyers refused to trade him to the Toronto Maple Leafs after he turned down their offer. Philadelphia would ultimately trade Lindros to the New York Rangers, where he would play the next three years, playing in 192 games while scoring 158 points on 66 goals and 92 assists. On August 11, 2005, Lindros signed a one-year deal with the Toronto, where he would score 22 points in 33 games.

**Becoming a Star**

Lindros signed a one-year contract with the Dallas Stars for the 2006–07 season on July 17, 2006. He played in 49 regular season games collecting 26 points with five goals and 21 assists. After eight concussions during his 13 year career, Lindros officially announced his retirement on November 8, 2007 at the age of 34.

## Gordie Howe – Hartford Whalers

CAREER HIGHLIGHTS

- Hall of Fame
- 6x Ross winner
- 6x Hart winner
- 21x All-Star
- 4x Cup winner

From 1946 to 1980, Gordon Howe played 26 seasons in the NHL and six in the WHL, with his first 25 seasons being spent with the Detroit Red Wings. Nicknamed "Mr. Hockey", Howe is considered by many as the most complete player to ever play the game and one of the greatest of all time.

Howe retired for the first time in 1971 and was inducted into the Hockey Hall of Fame the next year, but came back two years later to join his sons Mark and Marty on the Houston Aeros of the WHA. Although in his mid-40s, Howe scored over 100 points twice in six years, and was named most valuable player in 1974. In 1977, Howe signed as a free agent with the New England Whalers of the WHA.

At his final retirement in 1980, the right wing's 801 goals, 1,049 assists, and 1,850 total points were all NHL records that stood until they were broken by Wayne Gretzky several years later.

### BECOMING A WHALER

When the WHA folded in 1979, the New England Whalers joined the NHL as the renamed Hartford Whalers. While the Red Wings still held Howe's NHL rights, the teams reached an agreement in which Detroit agreed not to reclaim him. Howe played one final year in 1980, appearing in all 80 regular season games and helping Hartford make the playoffs by scoring 41 points (15 goals and 26 assists). At 52 years and 10 days, Howe became the oldest man to play an NHL game that post season.

## Guy Lafleur – Quebec Nordiques

CAREER HIGHLIGHTS

- Hall of Fame
- 3x Ross winner
- 3x Pearson winner
- 2x Hart winner
- 1x Smythe winner
- 8x All-Star

Guy Damien Lafleur was the first player in NHL history to score 50 goals as well as 50 goals and 100 points in six consecutive seasons, which he accomplished between 1974-75 and 1979-80.

Between 1971 and 1991, Lafleur played right wing for the Montreal Canadiens, New York Rangers, and Quebec Nordiques during an NHL career that spanned 17 seasons during which he would collect five Stanley Cup championships. At the age of 33, Lafleur decided to retire following the 1984-85 season after playing in only 19 games, and would be inducted into the NHL Hall-of-Fame in 1988.

A year after his induction, the 37 year-old Lafleur decided to unretire and signed a one-year contract with the New York Rangers. In 67 games, he would score 45 points with 18 goals and 27 assists. Lafleur was named one of the "100 Greatest NHL Players" in 2017.

### BECOMING AN NORDIQUE

After Rangers head coach and close friend Michel Bergeron was let go by New York, Lafleur followed him to the Quebec Nordiques for his final two seasons after reportedly turning down a $1 million offer from the Los Angeles Kings which would have allowed him to play alongside Wayne Gretzky. Lafleur managed 24 goals and 38 assists in 98 games with the Nordiques over the two seasons, while mentoring emerging star center Joe Sakic. The 39 year-old retired for good following the 1990-91 season.

## Jaromír Jágr – Calgary Flames

### Career Highlights

- Hall of Fame
- 5x Ross winner
- 3x Pearson winner
- 1x Hart winner
- 8x All-Star
- 2x Cup winner

Having played in 37 professional seasons (as of 2024), nine NHL teams and over 2,000 professional games, Jaromir Jágr has had the longest playing career in professional ice hockey history. Jágr has the second-most points in NHL history, after Wayne Gretzky. In 1990, at age 18, he was the youngest player in the NHL, and in 2017-18 was the oldest player when his NHL career ended. Jágr is also the oldest player to record a hat-trick.

In 806 games with the Pittsburgh Penguins, where he played 11 of his 24 seasons, Jágr became only the second player (after Mario Lemieux) to score 1,000 points as a Penguin. Jágr sits second behind Lemieux in career goals in franchise history and third in games played, assists and points.

### Becoming a Flame

On October 4 2017, Jágr, now 45 years old, signed a one-year contract with the Calgary Flames. The Flames were Jágr's ninth NHL team, but his first Canadian team.

On November 9, 2017 against the Detroit Red Wings, Jágr scored his first goal as a Flame, earning two points in a 6–3 win. However, injuries had limited Jágr to a career-low seven points in 22 games entering January 2018. On January 14, 2018, Jágr was placed on injured reserve, and on January 28 was placed on waivers, signaling the end of his brief tenure with the Flame.

After clearing waivers, the Flames assigned Jágr to Kladno of WSM Liga in the Czech National Hockey League. From 2018 through 2022, Jágr would play in 135 games for Kladno, scoring 82 points on 31 goals and 51 assists. In February 2023 he scored his 1,100th professional goal.

The 2023–24 season marked Jágr's 36th consecutive season of professional ice hockey, and on December 20, 2023, at the age of 51, Jágr played his first game of his 36th professional season, recording an assist in a 4–3 loss for Kladno.

## Larry Robinson – Los Angeles Kings

CAREER HIGHLIGHTS

- Hall of Fame
- 2x Norris winner
- 10x All-Star
- 6x Cup winner

Larry Clark Robinson played 17 seasons for the Montreal Canadiens and another three for the Los Angeles Kings, until his retirement after the 1991–92 season. He won the James Norris Memorial Trophy twice (1976–77 and 1979–80) as the league's most outstanding defenseman and won the Conn Smythe Trophy as the most valuable player of the 1978 playoffs.

During his career, Robinson played in 10 All-Star games and ended his 20-year career having scored 208 goals, 750 assists and 1,384 regular-season points as well as 144 points in 227 playoff games. Robinson holds the NHL record for most consecutive playoff seasons with 20, 17 of them with the Canadiens.

### BECOMING A KING

After 17 years with the Canadians, the 37 year-old Robinson signed a free agent contract with the Los Angeles Kings on July 26, 1989. In three seasons with the Kings, Robinson played in 182 games with 11 goals and 64 assists. In 1998, he was ranked number 24 on The Hockey News' list of the "100 Greatest Hockey Players". And in 2017, Robinson was named one of the "100 Greatest NHL Players".

## Paul Coffey – Boston Bruins

Career Highlights

- Hall of Fame
- 3x Norris winner
- 8x All-Star
- 4x Cup winner

Paul Douglas Coffey was drafted sixth overall by the Edmonton Oilers in the 1980 NHL Entry Draft. He blossomed in the 1981–82 season, scoring 89 points and was named a second-team NHL All-Star. In the Oilers' first Stanley Cup-winning season of 1983–84, he became only the second defenseman in NHL history to score 40 goals in a season and added 86 assists to finish second in point scoring. He won his first James Norris Memorial Trophy in 1984–85 while posting 37 goals and 121 points.

Coffey won the Norris Trophy again in 1985–86, while breaking Bobby Orr's record for goals in a season by a defenseman, scoring 48. His 138 points that year was second only to Orr's 139 in 1970–71 among defensemen. On December 22, 1990, Coffey became the second defenseman to record 1,000 points, doing so in a record-breaking 770 games. Coffey won a fourth Stanley Cup in 1990–91 with Pittsburgh. During the 1992 season Coffey passed Denis Potvin to become the career leader in goals, assists, and points by a defenseman. Ray Bourque of the Boston Bruins would break Coffey's records eight years later.

Becoming a Bruin

After stints in Pittsburgh, Los Angeles, Detroit, Hartford, Philadelphia and Chicago, Coffey signed with the Boston Bruins as a free agent in July, 2000. He was released on December 15 that year after playing in 18 games, scoring four points, all assists. He retired soon after at the age of 39.

## Ray Bourque – Colorado Avalanche

- Hall of Fame
- Calder Memorial trophy
- 5x Norris winner
- 1x Clancy winner
- 19x All-Star

During Raymond Jean Bourque's 21-year tenure with the Boston Bruins, he would help lead the team to a North American professional team record twenty-nine consecutive seasons in the playoffs, a streak that lasted through the 1996 season. In the playoffs, Bourque led the Boston to the Stanley Cup finals against the Edmonton Oilers in both 1988 and 1990, where the Bruins lost in both series.

It wouldn't be until 2000-01 as a member of the Colorado Avalanche that Bourque would win his first Stanley Cup. Bourque had waited longer to win his first Cup than any other Cup-winning player had in the 108-year history of the Stanley Cup, having played 1,612 regular season and 214 playoff games before winning his first trophy.

During the 2000–01 season, Bourque surpassed Paul Coffey to become the all-time leader in goals (410), assists (1,169) and points (1,579) for a defenseman in NHL history.

### BECOMING A RANGER

With his career nearing an end and the Bruins heading in the wrong direction, the 39 year-old Bourque requested a trade so he would have a chance to win a Stanley Cup. Bourque and fellow veteran Dave Andreychuk were sent to Colorado in exchange for three players and a first round draft choice on March 6, 2000. In two seasons in Colorado, Bourque played in 94 games, scoring 73 points on 15 goals and 58 assists.

## Wayne Gretzky – New York Rangers

Career Highlights

- Hall of Fame
- 10x Ross winner
- 9x Hart winner
- 5x Pearson winner
- 5x Byng winner
- 2x Smythe winner
- 15x All-Star

Wayne Douglas Gretzky played 20 seasons in the NHL for four teams from 1979 to 1999, 17 of those years with the Edmonton Oilers and Los Angeles Kings. He led the league in goal-scoring five times and assists 16 times, while winning four Stanley Cup titles and three Canada Cups.

Nicknamed "the Great One", Gretzky is the leading career goal scorer, assist producer and point scorer in NHL history, and has more career assists than any other player has total points. He is the only NHL player to total over 200 points in one season, a feat he accomplished four times. In addition, Gretzky scored over 100 points in 15 professional seasons, 13 of them consecutively. At the time of his retirement in 1999, Gretzky held 61 NHL records: 40 regular season records, 15 playoff records, and six All-Star records.

Hours after winning the 1988 Stanley Cup with Edmonton, Gretzky found out that he was being shopped around the league in an effort for Oilers ownership to shed costs. On  August 9, 1988 Gretzky was traded to the Kings in a blockbuster deal that shocked NHL fans and angered Oiler loyalists.

Eight years later, after three consecutive sub-.500 seasons with the Kings, Gretzky requested a trade to a contender, and was sent to the St. Louis Blues on February 27, 1996 for three players and two draft picks.

## BECOMING A RANGER

After one season in St. Louis, Gretzky rejected a three-year deal worth $15 million with the Blues, and instead signed a two-year, $8 million free agent contract with the New York Rangers, rejoining longtime Oilers teammate Mark Messier and former Kings teammate Luc Robitaille.

Gretzky ended his professional playing career with the Rangers after playing his final three seasons with them. In New York, Gretzky would score 249 points in 234 games, with 57 goals and 192 assists before retiring at the age of 38 in 1999.

## Primary Book Sources

- *MLB:*    https://www.baseball-reference.com/
- *NFL:*    https://www.pro-football-reference.com/
- *NBA:*    https://www.basketball-reference.com/
- *NHL:*    https://www.hockey-reference.com/

## Author's Bio

 Jeff Wagner is a native of the Bay Area in California, and has been a fan of Major League Baseball for over 50 years.

Jeff is a fan of all Bay Area sport teams, including the San Jose Sharks and Golden State Warriors, as well as teams from both the San Francisco and Oakland sides of the bay: San Francisco 49ers/Giants and the Oakland Raiders/A's, making him a dying breed as this is almost unheard of today in the Bay Area! Jeff has written several blogs on his experiences at drummerjeff.blogspot.com.

Jeff also likes playing the drums, and enjoys a blessed life with his wife Amy and their dog Lacey.

## More Books from the Author

**They Played Baseball for the Giants?**
*(ISBN-10: 1481931865 / ISBN-13: 978-1481931861)*

**They Played Baseball for the Yankees?**
*(ISBN-10: 161170295X / ISBN-13: 978-1611702958)*

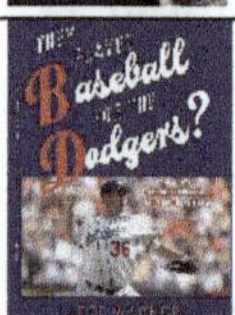

**They Played Baseball for the Dodgers?**
*(ISBN-10: 161170295X / ISBN-13: 978-1611702958)*

**They Played Baseball for the Red Sox?**
*(ISBN-13: 979-8726087047)*

**They Played Baseball for the Cubs?**
*(ISBN-13: 979-8502386821)*

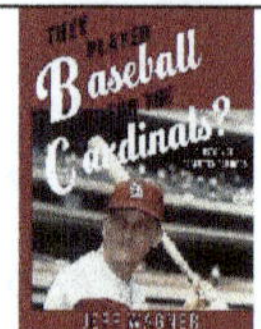

**They Played Baseball for the Cardinals?**
*(ISBN-13: 979-8472884877)*

**Willie the Met**
*(ISBN-13: 979-8372973886)*

**SF Bay Area Sports: 1970-2020: A Fan Revisits 50 Years of Amazing Sports Memories in the SF Bay Area**
*(ISBN-13: 979-8873789795)*

**Pug Shots: The Many Faces of a Chinese Pug**
*(ISBN-10: 1481931865 / ISBN-13: 978-1481931861)*

**CrossSearch Puzzles: A Trip Through the Bible – Book by Book -** *(ISBN-10: 161170295X / ISBN-13: 978-1611702958)*

**CrossSearch Puzzles: A Trip Through the Movies – Decade by Decade -** *(ISBN-13: 978-1479214587)*

9 798869 344274